What are ...?
VOLCANOES

www.heinemann.co.uk
Visit our website to find out more information about Heinemann Library books.

To order:
☎ Phone 44 (0) 1865 888066
🖷 Send a fax to 44 (0) 1865 314091
🖥 Visit the Heinemann Bookshop at www.heinemann.co.uk to browse our catalogue and order online.

First published in Great Britain by Heinemann Library,
Halley Court, Jordan Hill, Oxford OX2 8EJ,
a division of Reed Educational and Professional Publishing Ltd.
Heinemann is a registered trademark of Reed Educational and Professional Publishing Ltd.

OXFORD MELBOURNE AUCKLAND
JOHANNESBURG BLANTYRE GABORONE
IBADAN PORTSMOUTH (NH) USA CHICAGO

Designed by David Oakley
Illustrated by Hardlines and Jo Brooker
Originated by Dot Gradations
Printed by South China Printing in Hong Kong/China

ISBN 0 431 02439 1 (hardback)   ISBN 0 431 02444 8 (paperback)
05 04 03 02 01   05 04 03 02 01
10 9 8 7 6 5 4 3 2 1   10 9 8 7 6 5 4 3 2 1

British Library Cataloguing in Publication Data

Llewellyn, Claire
    What are volcanoes?. – (Take-off!)
    1.Volcanoes – Juvenile literature
    I.Title II.Volcanoes
    551.2'1

Acknowledgements
The publishers would like to thank the following for permission to reproduce photographs: Colorific!: Baron Sakiya p.12; FLPA: AA Riley p.5, A Nardi/Panda Photo p.26, USGS p.6, USDA Forest Service p.13, S Jonasson p.14, R Holcomb p.18, Jurgen & Christine Sohns p.20; NASA: Johnson Space Centre p.22, p.24; Oxford Scientific Films: Survival Anglia/Joan Root p.4, Frank Huber p.10, David B Fleetham p.15; Robert Harding Picture Library: Adina Tovy p.8, AC Waltham p.9, Kim Hart p.19, Tony Waltham p.21; Science Photo Library: NASA p.11; Still Pictures: Reinhard Janke p.16, John Cancalosi p.17; Trip: p.29, P Nicholas p.28.

Cover photograph reproduced with permission of FLPA.

Our thanks to Sue Graves and Hilda Reed for their advice and expertise in the preparation of this book.

Every effort has been made to contact copyright holders of any material reproduced in this book. Any omissions will be rectified in subsequent printings if notice is given to the publishers.

Contents

Any words appearing in the text in bold, **like this**, are explained in the Glossary.

What is a volcano?

Inside a volcano is a hole that goes down into the middle of the Earth. When it **erupts**, it shoots out red-hot liquid rock and ash from deep inside the Earth.

ash

liquid rock

Red-hot liquid rock and ash pour out of a volcano when it erupts.

Volcanoes are named after the Roman god of fire, Vulcan.

When the hot rock comes out of the volcano it is called **lava**. The lava then cools and hardens. This slowly builds the volcano up into a mountain. It may be years before the volcano erupts again.

solid lava

The sides of this volcano are made of solid lava.

What starts a volcano?

The Earth is made of rock. It is hard on the Earth's surface but hot and liquid underneath. The liquid rock squeezes out of holes in the Earth's surface.

Hot, liquid rock squeezes out from inside the Earth.

hot, liquid rock

One of the rocks that comes from lava is pumice. People use pumice to scrub their skin and make it smooth.

The top of the volcano is called the **crater**. The sides are called the **cone**.

A volcano is like a chimney with a large opening at the top. The hot, liquid rock is pushed up the chimney. When it **erupts**, the **lava** bursts out of the top and runs down the sides.

Building a volcano

steep sides

Mount Fuji in Japan has very steep sides.

Sometimes, the **lava** is so thick that it runs downhill very slowly. As it hardens, it builds a mountain with very steep sides.

Mount Fuji last erupted in 1707.

sloping sides

Mauna Loa on the island of Hawaii has gently sloping sides.

Sometimes, the lava is thin and runs downhill very fast. As it hardens, it builds a wider mountain with gentler slopes.

Lava can travel at up to 50 km an hour, much faster than a person can run!

Volcanoes in the sea

Many volcanoes rise up from the sea-bed. Each time they **erupt**, they grow a little higher until their peaks make islands in the sea.

island

This island is in Alaska. It is the top of an undersea volcano.

Sometimes a line of undersea volcanoes grows above the surface of the water. Their peaks make a long line of islands in the sea called an island arc.

A long line of islands is called an island arc.

Different eruptions

Volcanoes that **erupt** regularly are called **active** volcanoes. Some erupt gently. The **lava** seeps out quietly and the gas comes out in puffs.

gas

lava

The Mauna Loa volcano in Hawaii erupts quietly.

Mauna Loa has lots of craters. It also has the second largest active crater in the world.

Mount St Helens in the USA erupted violently in 1980.

Other volcanoes erupt like a bomb going off. Sometimes, a part of the mountain may be destroyed. Part of the **cone** of Mount St Helens in the USA was blown away.

After Mount St Helens exploded, its height was reduced from 2950 metres to 2560 metres.

The power of volcanoes

Volcanoes have a sudden and deadly power. The hot **lava** can destroy towns and kill people. The ash from the volcano can crush houses and plants.

volcano

ash

Ash from this volcano has buried these houses.

When Krakatoa **erupted** in 1883, it was heard 4000 km away.

lava

road

This stream of lava is flowing over a road. Nothing can stop it.

When lava pours out of a volcano, it burns everything in its path. It flattens trees and crops, and covers the land.

Sometimes lumps of lava cool and become hard as they shoot through the air. They are called 'bombs'.

Using volcanoes

These fields lie at the foot of a volcano in Spain.

volcano

Volcanoes can be very useful. The ash and lava make the ground very good for farming. Crops grow well in the soil on the slopes.

The soil formed from volcanic ash and lava is full of **minerals**. It also holds water very well.

The rocks near volcanoes are often very hot. Power stations use them to heat water. This helps them to make electricity for factories and homes.

The heat from volcanoes is used to make steam to drive machines.

Volcanic rock contains heat from the Earth.

Studying volcanoes

Scientists who study volcanoes are called **vulcanologists**. They measure volcanoes and check for movements in the ground.

vulcanologist

This vulcanologist is measuring how fast the **lava** is moving.

lava

observatory

Scientists work in this **observatory** on a volcano.
It is in Hawaii.

Scientists learn lots of things from studying
volcanoes. They use the results to try to predict
when a volcano will next **erupt**. This could
save many people's lives.

Vulcanologists wear special clothing, to
protect them from the heat, when they take
samples of lava and gas from volcanoes.

Old volcanoes

Volcanoes that have not **erupted** for many years are called **dormant** volcanoes. We sometimes say they are sleeping.

Mount Kilimanjaro

Mount Kilimanjaro in Kenya, Africa, is a dormant volcano.

The word *dormant* comes from the French word meaning 'sleeping'.

The sides of this volcano have been worn away by wind and rain over thousands of years.

Volcanoes that will never erupt again are called **extinct** volcanoes. Their **cones** are slowly worn down by the weather.

The rock left behind like this is called a lava plug.

Volcano map 1

sea

volcano

This photo of a volcano was taken by a satellite above the Earth.

This is a photo of a volcano. It was taken by a **satellite** high above the Earth. The volcano is an island just off the coast. It is surrounded by sea.

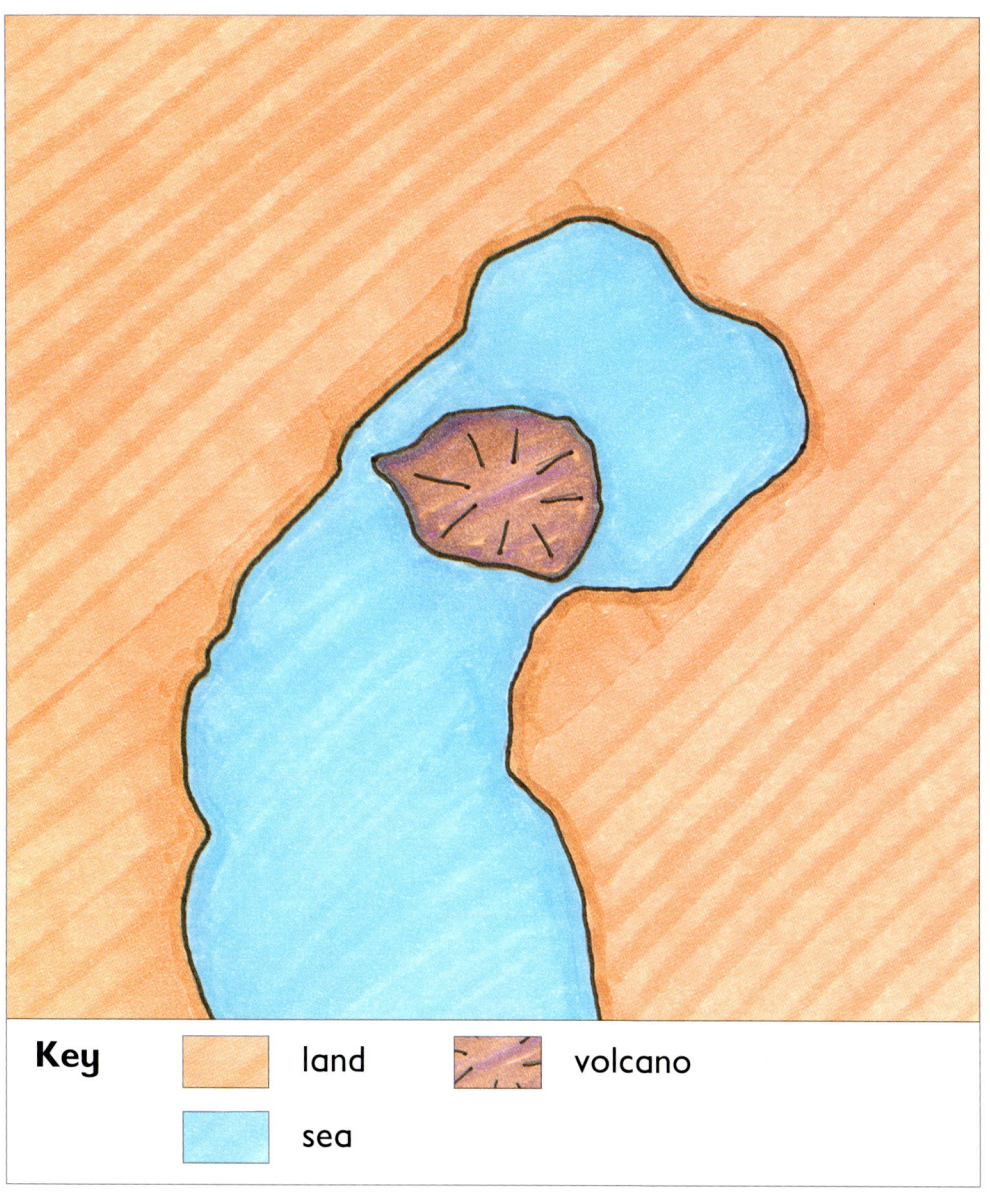

Key

land · volcano

sea

This map shows us the same place as the photo.
The key tells us what each colour means.

23

Volcano map 2

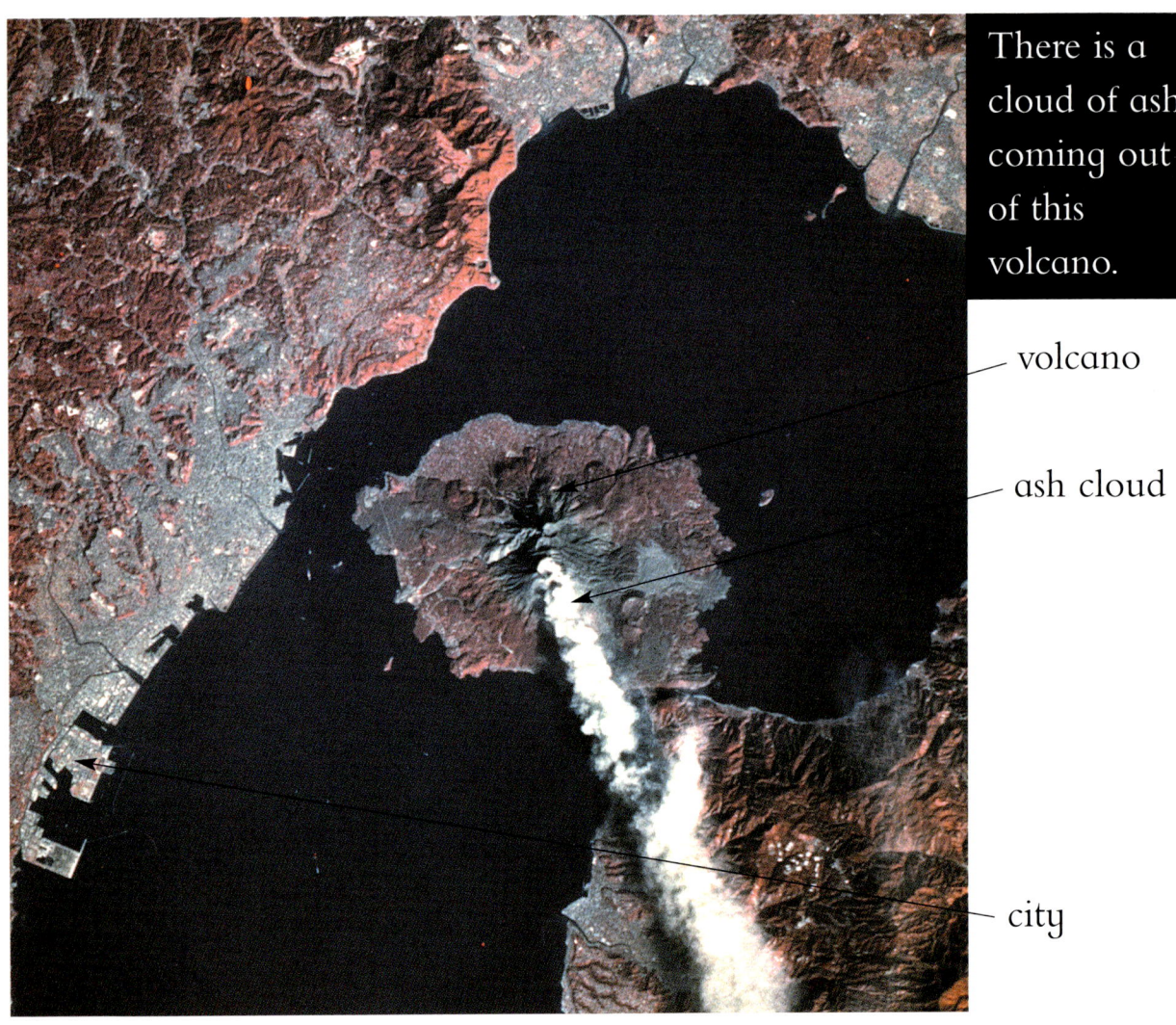

There is a cloud of ash coming out of this volcano.

volcano

ash cloud

city

This photo shows a smaller part of the land but you can see it more clearly. The volcano looks bigger. You can see a cloud of ash coming out of it. You can see a city on the coast.

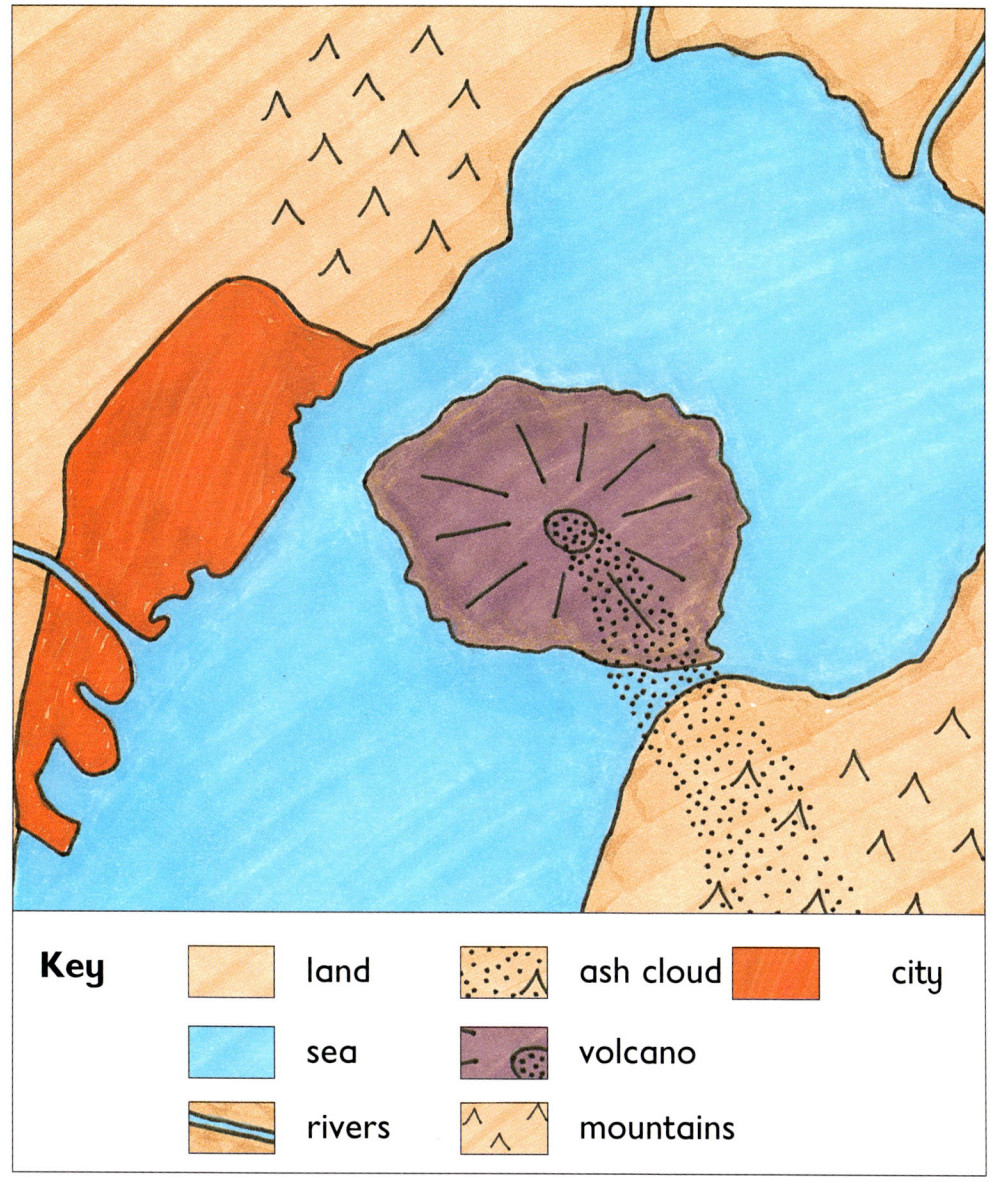

Key

land	ash cloud		city
sea	volcano		
rivers	mountains		

On this map, the red colour shows the buildings in the city. The black dots show ash coming out of the volcano.

Volcano map 3

crater

You can see inside the crater of this volcano.

This photo shows another volcano. It was taken from an aeroplane. It does not show the whole volcano, but you can see inside the **crater** very clearly.

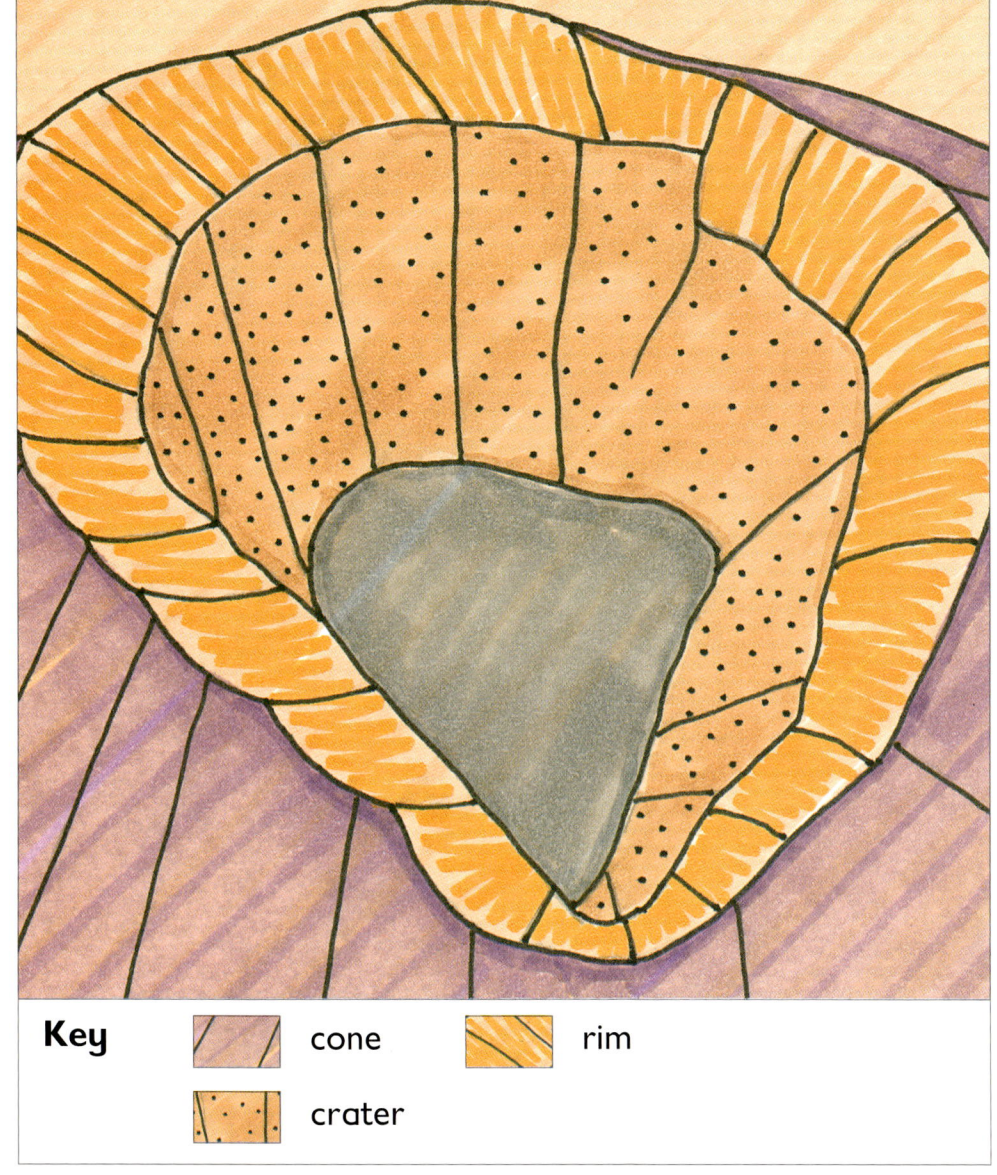

Key   ⬚ cone   ⬚ rim   ⬚ crater

The **cone** of the volcano is very steep. At the rim of the crater, the land sinks down steeply to the middle.

Amazing volcano facts

About 2000 years ago, Mount Vesuvius in Italy suddenly **erupted**. It buried the Roman town of Pompeii. You can visit the ruins of the town.

town ruins

Mount Vesuvius

Mount Vesuvius buried Pompeii when it erupted 2000 years ago.

Mount Vesuvius last erupted in 1944. Work out how long ago that was.

observatory

Mauna Kea is the top of an undersea volcano.

Mauna Kea, an island in Hawaii, is the top of an undersea volcano. An **observatory** has been built on the island.

Mauna Kea measures 10,205 metres from the sea-bed to the peak.

Glossary

a b c d e f g h i j k l m n o p q r s t u v w x y z

active able to erupt

cone sides of a volcano

crater large round opening at the top of a volcano

dormant has not erupted for many years

erupt suddenly shoot out lava and ash

extinct will never erupt again

lava hot, liquid rock that shoots out of a volcano from inside the Earth

mineral a substance in soil that can help keep living things healthy

observatory special building where people like scientists can watch a volcano and make measurements

satellite special machine in space which goes round the Earth and can take photographs

vulcanologist person who studies volcanoes

More books to read

Daniel Rogers.

Geography Starts Here! Volcano.

Wayland, 1998

Claire Llewellyn.

Why do we have... Rocks and Mountains?

Heinemann, 1997

Andy Owen and Miranda Ashwell.

What Are... Mountains?

Heinemann, 1998

Daphne Butler.

What Happens when Volcanoes Erupt?

Simon and Schuster, 1993

Index

active 7, 12

ash 4, 8, 14, 16, 24, 25

cone 7, 13, 21, 27

crater 7, 12, 26, 27

dormant 15, 20

erupt 4, 5, 7, 8, 10, 12, 13, 14, 19, 20, 21, 28

extinct 21

farming 16

island arc 11

lava 5, 7, 8, 9, 12, 14, 15, 16, 18, 19, 21

maps 23, 25, 27

undersea volcanoes 10, 11, 29

volcano uses 17

vulcanologist 18, 19